LIBRA

THE ARTFUL ASTROLOGER

LIBRA

Lee Holloway

Gramercy Books
New York • Avenel

To my children

A Friedman Group Book

Copyright ©1993 by Michael Friedman Publishing Group

This 1993 edition is published by Gramercy Books,
distributed by Outlet Book Company, Inc.,
a Random House Company, 40 Engelhard Avenue,
Avenel, New Jersey 07001.

Printed and bound in Singapore

Library of Congress Cataloging–in–Publication Data

    Holloway, Lee.
        The artful astrologer.   Libra / by Lee Holloway.
            p.   cm.
        ISBN 0-517-08256-X
        1. Libra (Astrology)   I. Title.
      BF1727.45H65   1993
      133.5'2—dc20   93-24864
                                      CIP

8 7 6 5 4 3 2 1

CONTENTS

Symbolic rendering of a seventeenth-century astrologer.

INTRODUCTION

Is astrology bunk, or is there something to it? If astrology is utter nonsense, why have so many of the world's finest thinkers, including Johannes Kepler, Copernicus, Isaac Newton, Carl Jung, and Goethe, turned to astrology for information and guidance over the centuries?

Some people may scoff when astrology is mentioned, but even these skeptics are usually inquisitive about their signs. Whenever I attend a dinner party, I ask the host not to mention that I am an astrologer—at least not until dessert—because the conversation invariably turns to astrolo-

In the middle ages, the wealthy consulted astrologers regularly.

gy. When people learn that I am an astrologer, they first try to get me to tell them about their signs and what lies in store for them. Then, in a subtle way, they bring up the next bit of business, which usually concerns a loved one. Finally, as you've probably guessed, they want to know whether the two signs get along.

We humans are an inquisitive lot—we are eager to learn more about our friends, family, lovers, and employers. Astrology is one way to satisfy that natural curiosity.

In the not too distant past, only royalty, heads of state, and the very rich consulted with astrologers; such consultation was a privilege of the elite. Today, astrology is a source of information and fascination for millions; astrological columns can be found in major newspapers and magazines all over the world.

Astrology is not a form of magic. It is a science. Put simply, it is a practical application of astronomy that links the stars and planets with our daily lives. A horoscope is a picture of the stars and planets at a given time, such as that of a person's birth. By examining each planet's position and the relationships of all of the planets to each other at a specific moment, an astrologer can determine your basic personality or predict a general course of events. Perhaps the noted Swiss psychologist Carl Jung summed up the concept of astrology best when he said, "Whatever is born or done at this moment, has the qualities of this moment in time." Astrologers form a continuous link with the past, and each human being, although unique, is part of nature and the universe.

Unfortunately, some people have the misconception that astrology dictates who they are and how their life has to be.

This chart dates back to fourteenth-century Italy. The inside circles represent the element, ruling body part, and orientation of each respective sign.

Medieval illuminated manuscript of biblical characters observing the stars.

Nothing could be further from the truth. Astrology does not remove our free will; it simply points out our basic nature and how we are likely to react in certain circumstances. Astrology indicates strengths and weaknesses, talents and abilities, difficulties and opportunities. It is always up to the individual to use this information, and to live his or her life accordingly, or to disregard it.

Like other sciences, astrology's origins date back thousands of years. There is evidence that primitive peoples recorded the phases of the Moon by carving notches on reindeer bones, and that they may have linked the Moon's movement with the tides, or the snow's melting in spring with the rising of the constellation now known as Aries. As early as 2000 B.C., astrologers were using instruments—carved out of granite or fashioned from brass or copper—to observe and calculate the positions of constellations. These calculations were surprisingly accurate, even by today's standards.

Over time, astrological calculations were refined and the planets were named. The Babylonians were the first to describe the natural zodiac, and their first horoscope dates back to 409 B.C. Centuries ago, people began to examine the stars' potential impact on human emotions, spirit, and intellect. Today, astrology is so deeply embedded in our culture and language that we rarely give it a second thought. The

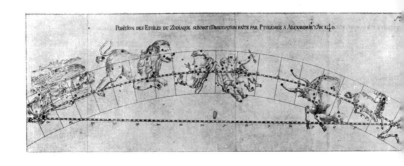

The twelve zodiacal constellations as drawn according to Ptolemy's descriptions.

days of the week , for example, have their roots in astrology. Sunday is derived from "Sun Day," Monday from "Moon Day," Tuesday from "Tiwe's Day," Wednesday from "Woden's Day," Thursday from "Thor's Day," Friday from "Frigga's Day," and Saturday from "Saturn's Day." Lunacy, which originally referred to so-called full-moon madness, now encompasses all varieties and forms of mental illness.

Before we begin, I'd like to touch upon one final point. Throughout this book, you'll see references to "rulers." A ruler, in astrological terms, has the same meaning as it does in human society; "ruler" refers to the planet that governs or co-governs an astrological sign (see pages 14–15) or to the constellation rising at the birth of a person or event. Everything has a moment of birth: people, places, profes-

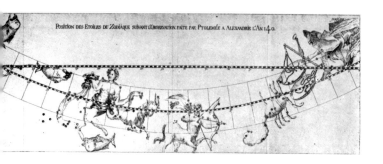

POSITION DES ETOILES DU ZODIAQUE SUIVANT L'OBSERVATION FAITE PAR PTOLEMÉE A ALEXANDRIE L'AN 140.

sions, even ideas; it would take volumes to show you what persons, places, and things your sign rules, but a small sampling has been included here. For example, different parts of the body have rulers, and that body part is often a point of strength and weakness. Gemstones and colors have also been assigned to each sign, although there are varying opinions about the validity of these less important areas. (It should also be noted here that the gemstone assigned to a particular sign does not correspond to the birthstone assigned to that month.) Generally, however, colors and gemstones are said to reflect the specific energy of each sign.

May *The Artful Astrologer* enlighten and entertain you.

Lee Holloway

THE PLANETS

The **SUN** symbolizes the life force that flows through everything. It rules the sign of Leo and represents ego, will, identity, and consciousness.

The **MOON** symbolizes emotions and personality. It rules the sign of Cancer and represents feeling, instinct, habit, childhood, mother, sensitivity, and receptivity.

MERCURY symbolizes the mind and communication. It rules the signs of Gemini and Virgo and represents thought, learning, communication, reason, speech, youth, and perception.

VENUS symbolizes love and attraction. It rules the signs of Taurus and Libra and represents harmony, values, pleasure, comfort, beauty, art, refinement, and balance.

MARS symbolizes action and drive. It rules the sign of Aries and represents energy, the sex drive, initiative, the ability to defend oneself, resilience, and conflict.

JUPITER symbolizes expansion and growth. It rules the sign of Sagittarius and represents higher thought and learning, principles, beliefs, optimism, abundance, idealism, and morals.

SATURN symbolizes universal law and reality. It rules the sign of Capricorn and represents structure, discipline, limitation, restriction, fear, authority figures, father, teachers, and time.

The nine planets that comprise our solar system: Mercury, Venus, Earth, Mars, Saturn, Jupiter, Uranus, Neptune, and Pluto.

URANUS symbolizes individuality and change. It rules the sign of Aquarius and represents intuition, genius, insight, reform, unconventionality, and freedom.

NEPTUNE symbolizes compassion and spirituality. It rules the sign of Pisces and represents the search for the divine, intuition, dreams, illusion, imagination, and confusion.

PLUTO symbolizes transformation and regeneration. It rules the sign of Scorpio and represents power, death and rebirth, the subconscious, elimination, obsession, and purging.

THE ZODIAC SIGNS

Just as there are twelve months in the year, there are twelve astrological signs in the zodiac. The word "zodiac" comes from the Greek *zoidiakos*, which means "circle of animals" and refers to a band of fixed stars that encircles the earth. The twelve signs are divided into four elements: fire, air, earth, and water. The three signs within an element share many similarities, but each sign in the zodiac is unique. The following section is a brief summary of the qualities of the signs born under each element. (The terms "positive" and "negative" as they are used here describe qualities, and are not judgments.)

The fire signs are Aries, Leo, and Sagittarius. They are termed positive and extroverted. They are warm, creative, outgoing, expressive, idealistic, inspirational, and enthusiastic.

The air signs are Gemini, Libra, and Aquarius. They are termed positive and extroverted. They are social, outgoing, objective, expressive, and intellectual.

The earth signs are Taurus, Virgo, and Capricorn. They are termed negative and introverted. They are practical, conservative, reserved, traditional, and deliberate.

The water signs are Cancer, Scorpio, and Pisces. They are termed negative and introverted. They are sensitive, emotional, imaginative, and intuitive.

The fire signs:

Aries   Leo   Sagittarius

The air signs:

Gemini   Libra   Aquarius

The earth signs:

Taurus   Virgo   Capricorn

The water signs:

Cancer   Scorpio   Pisces

L i b

Symbol: Scales

Planetary ruler: Venus

Element: Air

Rules in the body: Kidneys

Day of the week: Friday

Gem: Jade

Color: Blue-green

Key words: I balance

r a

YOUR SUN SIGN PROFILE

In a meeting, at a restaurant, or at any social gathering, the person who introduces everyone to each other or checks the room to see who's feeling left out is probably a Libra. Libras just can't help themselves when it comes

CITIES RULED BY LIBRA

Antwerp, Belgium
Copenhagen, Denmark
Friebourg, Switzerland
Leeds, England
Lisbon, Portugal
Vienna, Austria

A beautiful nighttime view of the Vienna skyline.

to trying to make others feel good. In their world, life is one enormous "we," so they're somewhat tied to the notion that if someone is not happy, they

have to fix it. This attractive and usually very bright sign is a born

people-pleaser. It's not that surprising, for Venus, the goddess of love, is Libra's ruler and the scales of justice is the sign's astrological symbol.

Libras strive to create harmony in every aspect of their lives. After all, their key words, "I balance," are their motivating force. Certainly they are charming and gracious, but more importantly, they are constantly trying to make life fair. Libras are impartial and have a great talent for seeing all sides of a question (more judges and lawyers are born under this sign than any other), but unfortunately, this talent often results in difficulty making decisions.

When it comes to decision making, Libras have the potential to exhaust themselves—and everyone else around them. They will finally seem to come to a decision, and then just when it appears that everything has been resolved, they're off again, weighing and ana-

LIBRA MYSTERY MAKERS

John le Carré
Ellery Queen

Truman Capote

lyzing. Although they put themselves through the ringer mentally and emotionally, this is one sign you'll never see sweat or, in Libra vernacular, glisten. Outwardly, Libras are cool, calm, and collected. They were born to handle this type of juggling act. They seem to take everything in stride. At times, their charm and diplomacy can be almost maddening, but every once in a very great while, when they're pressed to the wall, a little stress shows through their lovely exterior—not much, just enough to confirm their humanity and relieve any feelings of inadequacy others may have by comparison.

As for their professional lives, Libras work just where you'd expect them to, in jobs that range from public rela-

ASTRONOMICAL FACT

Venus, planetary ruler of Libra, is almost the exact size of the Earth. Because Venus is covered by dense clouds, it has a beautiful soft appearance and is brightly lit. Its axis rotation is backward, and it takes this planet almost 243 days to orbit the Sun.

tions to diplomacy; their natural ability to calm troubled waters makes them well suited to interact with the public and mediate between adversaries. Their love of beauty leads many Libras to pursue careers in fashion, design, and the arts. Above all, Libras thrive in work situations that involve partnership or teamwork.

Of all the zodiac signs, Libra has the most difficulty standing alone. Libras were born to share both their professional and personal lives with someone. They actually seem to need to share everything. When it comes to romance, no one can quite match Libra's instincts for pleasing others. This talent, coupled with strong personal appeal (Yves Montand was a Libra, as is Julio Iglesias), gives Libra the ability to set a romantic mood with a minimal amount of effort—an empty room, a stool, and a couple of candles will do. In many ways, Libra epitomizes the word "romance."

Like every sign, Libra has positive and negative attributes and the ability to choose which qualities to express. As a Libra, you should recognize that people-pleasing carried to an extreme can lead to dishonesty and deception, and that it's important to be clear about your own needs and feelings. You may have to be aware that saying what others want to hear works only if what you're saying is true, and that if you use your charm as a manipulative device, it will undermine your own sense of self-esteem. You also must try to take a firm position on matters as quickly as

Dizzy Gillespie

you can to spare yourself—and others—emotional wear and tear.
Sometimes it's best to make a decision
and act on it until making other changes becomes necessary.
With so many talents and fine attributes, the few lessons you may
need to learn in decisiveness and straightforwardness will go a
long way in helping you achieve your goals.

Bardot

COMPATIBILITY WITH THE OTHER SIGNS

In nature, some elements are more compatible and blend more easily than others, like fire and air, and earth and water; the same holds true in astrology. Therefore, some astrological signs naturally interact more harmoniously than others.

The information in this section describes how Libra relates to each of the other signs. It provides guidelines to the potential strengths and weaknesses of a relationship between two signs. But remember, these are only guidelines. In the final analysis, the choice is yours.

As an air sign, Libra is most compatible with the other air signs, Gemini and Aquarius. The natural rapport of the air signs stems from their many emotional and intellectual similarities.

> **GIFTS SURE TO PLEASE LIBRAS**
>
> A romantic getaway for two; sentimental cards; recordings of favorite music; subscriptions to interior design, fashion, or gardening magazines; anything blue-green

The fire signs Leo and Sagittarius are favorable partners for Libra, too. Although Aries is also a fire sign, it is Libra's opposite in the zodiac, so the relationship would be a bit more challenging than one with the other fire signs. In nature "air fans fire, and fire warms air," and the same holds true in astrology. This is the reason air and fire signs are basically compatible.

The earth signs—Taurus, Virgo, and Capricorn—are not as compatible with Libra as the fire and air signs, since earth signs tend to lack the sociability and adventurousness that attracts Libra. Earth signs are also quite practical and may find it difficult to contend with Libra's changeable and indecisive nature.

The water signs—Cancer, Scorpio, and Pisces—also represent less suitable candidates for Libra because of their basic elemental differences. Water signs tend to look at the world from a deeply emotional perspective, which could be exasperating for Libra, who feels that all problems can be solved by making a rational list of pros and cons.

GEMINI AND LIBRA

 Gemini (May 22–June 21) and Libra can make an exciting match. Both are intellectual signs, but they differ in their approaches to life. Libra needs to please others and to weigh and balance matters before making a final decision; Gemini is a nonconformist who can make several different decisions, ultimately following the one that seems most likely to work. Libra is very concerned with appearances, and has natural style and grace. Gemini is more interested in verbal exchanges than in fashion and often lacks tact. But even with these differences, the two signs will probably get along. Libra will discover new ideas, people, and places thanks to curious Gemini, while Gemini will benefit from Libra's natural diplomacy and charm.

**LIBRA ACTORS WHO
DISPLAY THEIR SIGN'S
GREAT VERSATILITY**

Karen Allen
Catherine Deneuve
Lillian Gish
Charlton Heston
Glynis Johns
Rita Hayworth
Angela Lansbury
Carole Lombard
Marcello Mastroianni
Walter Matthau
Yves Montand
Christopher Reeve
Susan Sarandon
George C. Scott

Sigourney Weaver

AQUARIUS AND LIBRA

Aquarius (January 20–
February 18) and Libra
are also highly suitable
partners. Aquarius, however, is a
real rebel, often involved in new
reforms or causes, while Libra, a
peacemaker, is always seeking
harmony. Unlike Libra, Aquarius prefers to remain
unattached. In fact, Libra may meet with some resistance in
trying to get a firm commitment from elusive, freedom-lov-
ing Aquarius. But Libra can charm almost anyone in order
to get what he or she wants, and Aquarius is certainly not
indifferent. Both signs love to socialize, which can add a
level of excitement to the relationship.

LIBRA AND LIBRA

Two Libras can form a successful relationship
because of their similar natures; it's easy to under-
stand someone who is so much like yourself.
However, Libra is notorious for flirting and indecisiveness,
a difficult combination for anyone to handle—even another
Libra. When two Libras are brought together, the union
amplifies their mutual weaknesses, making it difficult for
either partner to balance the other's shortcomings. If both

A perfect example of a dazzling Libra-Aquarius combination is Carole Lombard (Libra) and Clark Gable (Aquarius). Although their marriage was brief because of her tragically early death, together they enchanted the world. She was a true Libra, a beauty with style, grace, and a wonderful sense of humor. Independent, magnetic, and charming (Aquarian qualities), Gable often played romantic leads, although some of his greatest roles made the audience laugh long and hard. The obvious chemistry between the couple is indicative of the potential attraction that these two signs hold for each other.

partners can address these issues honestly, they may be able to work things out—and what a charming pair they will make.

LEO AND LIBRA

Leo (July 24–August 23) and Libra: even the sound of their names fairly sings. The blending of their two ruling planets, the Sun and Venus, is one of the hap-

Susan Sarandon and Tim Robbins are a good example of a successful relationship between two Libras. True partner-oriented Libras, these two appear not only to be deeply devoted to each other and their two children,

but also to affect each other's lives on many other levels. As actors, they have enriched and contributed to each others' careers, appearing together in feature films, including Robbins' directorial debut, *Bob Roberts*. In keeping with their sign's concern for justice, the two have also been involved in furthering many political causes, most notably women's and animal rights.

piest planetary combinations possible. Leo is affectionate, open, and faithful, while Libra entices, charms, and instinctively responds to Leo's need for lots of attention. Both signs rule affairs of the heart, romance, and marriage. No one has more flair than Leo,

but Libra brings a personal bit of magic to this union. If these two get together, they will almost certainly have a successful relationship.

SAGITTARIUS AND LIBRA

 The combination of Sagittarius (November 22–December 21) and Libra unites two of the most beneficial planets in the heavens, Venus and Jupiter. Sagittarius is one of the most expansive signs of the zodiac and is naturally outgoing, optimistic, and decisive. Libra tends to put others' personal wants and needs before his or her own, and adaptable Sagittarius is also something of a people-pleaser, and will generally be able to get Libra to act on his or her true desires. Sagittarius' happy nature can be infectious for Libra, who often acts more cool and reserved than he or she really feels. Sagittarius can help Libra to be more decisive, and Libra can teach Sagittarius to be more diplomatic, which is not a bad trade-off.

John Lennon

ARIES AND LIBRA

Aries (March 21–April 20) opposes Libra in the zodiac—and opposites do attract in astrology. Libra is cool and objective, carefully weighing all opinions before making a decision. Aries is excitable, decisive, and highly impulsive. While Libra thinks in terms of "we," Aries thinks in terms of "I." Because the Arian approach is so direct, an Aries will often have to backtrack to clean up the chaos he or she has caused; in contrast, Libra can measure matters for so long that the chance to choose is almost lost. Aries is emotional, while Libra is rational. This twosome can balance each other, but only if they accept and adjust to their differences.

TAURUS AND LIBRA

A union between Taurus (April 21–May 21) and Libra certainly has great potential. Both are ruled by Venus, which means these two are quite pleasure-oriented. However, earthy Taurus may be a bit too unrefined for more sophisticated Libra. Taurus' expression of passion is more

SOME COUNTRIES RULED BY LIBRA

Argentina
Burma
China
Japan
Tibet

Mount Fuji as seen from Lake Ashinoko, Japan.

Libras have strong social and mediating skills, and thus are often considered the hosts of the zodiac, a role well suited to former late-night television host Johnny Carson.

physical, while Libra's is more intellectual. Taurus also prefers familiar surroundings when socializing, while Libra is at home in almost any setting. These two have a chance—but not without compromise and adjustment.

VIRGO AND LIBRA

 Virgo (August 24–September 22) and Libra both approach life from an intellectual stance and would probably never be at a loss for conversation, although Virgo is more critical and analytical. Virgo is shy and less comfortable in the social settings that Libra needs and enjoys. Libra is outgoing and needs to interact with others to spark his or her own energy, and this factor could be a major hurdle for a relationship between these two signs.

CAPRICORN AND LIBRA

 Capricorn (December 22–January 19) and Libra is another combination that has its work cut out for it. Capricorn is reserved and prefers social gatherings that pertain to business, while Libra finds socializing pleasurable no matter what the occasion. Both of these signs present a cool exterior, but the similarity ends there. For Libra, life needs to be fair, and preferably elegant, while practical Capricorn tends to focus less on style and more on content. Libra also needs to share, while Capricorn is quite independent. These two have some real differences that may prove difficult to accommodate over the long term. But if they are mature and can accept each other's differences, they may be able to make the relationship work.

SOME PROFESSIONS RULED BY LIBRA
actor
artist
beautician
cosmetician
dancer
designer
diplomat
florist
furrier
interior decorator
jeweler
judge
juggler
lawyer
milliner
musician
negotiator
painter
tailor
wigmaker

CANCER AND LIBRA

 Cancer (June 22–July 23) is a sensitive sign, awash in emotional highs and lows, and Libra is not fond of heavy emotional scenes. Libra asks "What do you think?" Cancer asks "How do you feel?" These very different approaches are the basis of the personalities of these signs, which could make it hard for either to compromise. While both signs desire love and a family, in the end, Libra's objectivity may be difficult for Cancer to comprehend and Cancer's mood-

Libra Thomas Wolfe's novel You Can't Go Home Again *reflects the great social awareness and intellectual orientation of his sign.*

As Venus rules the arts in all its forms, it's no surprise that many creative people—Christopher Reeve, Jim Henson, George Gershwin, and Bob Geldof— were born under the sign of Venus-ruled Libra.

iness may simply be too much for Libra. However, Libra can lend some rationality to moody Cancer, while Cancer is a dependable, nurturing choice for partner-oriented Libra.

SCORPIO AND LIBRA

 Scorpio (October 23–November 21) and Libra is perhaps the most challenging pairing of the air-water combinations. Libra's need to share everything—ideas, dreams, and friends—could be difficult for Scorpio. Scorpio are deeply private and can be selfish, so sharing is a concept that is hard for them to grasp. Scorpios can be giving, but usually only on his or her terms—quite unlike Libra, whose main function is to please others and keep harmony. Libra could experience a lot of difficulty in this union, for the burden of the relationship will most likely fall on his or her shoulders since Scorpio is extremely stubborn, as well as unable and often unwilling to change.

PISCES AND LIBRA

 Pisces (February 19–March 20) and Libra can make some very strange music together. Each has the potential to present an almost ethereal presence. Both are signs that attract others, but their ruling planets, Venus and Neptune, give each sign a different kind of allure.

Pisces is gentle, emotional, shy, and inclined to worry; Libra is charming, outgoing, and changeable. Because Pisces' head and feet are often in the clouds or in his or her own world of imagination, this sign is not the best source of objectivity. Because of this and Pisces' tendency to worry, Libra would do better to bounce decisions off someone who is better grounded. At the same time, Pisces may find Libra's intellectual approach too detached for his or her liking. However, these two could make an interesting pair, if both partners acknowledge the problems inherent to the relationship and take steps to overcome them.

Remember, astrology's compatibility guidelines do not mean that one sign can't have a good relationship with another. They merely indicate areas where there is potential for harmony, and areas that will require patience, adjustment, and acceptance.

Julio Iglesias possesses the typical Libran good looks and ear for harmony; he clearly identifies with being a Libra, too, for he titled one of his albums after the sign.

BIRTHDAYS OF FAMOUS LIBRAS

Bruce Springsteen

September 23

Bruce Springsteen
Augustus Caesar • Julio Iglesias
Mickey Rooney • Les McCann

September 24

F. Scott Fitzgerald
Jim Henson • George Raft
Joseph P. Kennedy III

Michael Douglas

September 25

Michael Douglas • Christopher Reeve •
William Faulkner • Barbara Walters

September 26

George Gershwin • Bryan Ferry
T. S. Eliot • Olivia Newton-John

September 27

Cyril Scott • Arthur Penn
Wilford Brimley • Meatloaf

Barbara Walters

September 28

Brigitte Bardot • William S. Paley
Marcello Mastroianni

Marcello Mastroianni

September 29

Michelangelo Antonioni • Gene Autry • Anita Ekberg • Greer Garson

September 30

Truman Capote • Angie Dickinson
Deborah Kerr • Johnny Mathis

October 1

Mary McFadden • Vladimir Horowitz
Walter Matthau • Julie Andrews
Grete Waitz

Olivia Newton-John

October 2

Mahatma Mohandas Gandhi
Sting • Don McLean

Patti LaBelle

October 3

Gore Vidal • Eddie Cochran
Emily Post • Chubby Checker
Thomas Wolfe

October 4

Jean Millet • Charlton Heston • Susan Sarandon • Patti LaBelle

October 5

Bob Geldof • Glynis Johns • Karen Allen • Vaclav Havel

October 6

Carole Lombard • Thor Heyerdahl • Britt Ekland • Jenny Lind

October 7

Desmond Tutu • Oliver North • June Allyson
Yo Yo Ma • R.D. Laing

October 8

David Carradine • Sigourney Weaver
Chevy Chase • Juan Perón

*Thelonious
Monk*

October 9

John Lennon • Sean Lennon
Miguel de Cervantes • Jackson Browne

*Martina
Navratilova*

October 10

Thelonious Monk • Harold Pinter • Martina Navratilova
Giuseppe Verdi • David Lee Roth

October 11

Eleanor Roosevelt • Art Blakey • Jerome Robbins

October 12

Luciano Pavarotti • Aleister Crowley • Susan Anton • Dick Gregory

October 13

Paul Simon • Margaret Thatcher
Yves Montand• Nipsey Russell

Lillian Gish

October 14

Roger Moore • Lillian Gish • e.e. cummings
Ralph Lauren

October 15

Friedrich W. Nietzsche • Penny Marshall • Oscar Wilde
Arthur Schlesinger, Jr. • Mario Puzo

Oscar Wilde

October 16

Eugene O'Neill • Noah Webster • Angela Lansbury • Gunter Grass

October 17

Rita Hayworth • Montgomery Clift • Arthur Miller • Evel Knievel

October 18

Wynton Marsalis • Melina Mercouri • Chuck Berry • George C. Scott

October 19

John le Carré • Jennifer Holiday • Peter Max

October 20

Ellery Queen • Art Buchwald • Tom Petty • Mickey Mantle

October 21

Carrie Fisher • Samuel Taylor Coleridge
Dizzy Gillespie • Ursula K. LeGuin

October 22

Franz Liszt • Catherine Deneuve
Robert Rauschenberg

October 23

Johnny Carson • Pelé

Wynton Marsalis

Jennifer Holliday

ABOUT THE AUTHOR

Lee Holloway has been a practicing astrologer with an international clientele for more than fifteen years. The author of a series of comprehensive astrology engagement calendars, she has hosted her own television and radio programs, including her current show on KABC Talk Radio in Los Angeles. A Sagittarius and the mother of three, she lives in Woodland Hills, California.

PHOTO CREDITS